# BOTTICELLI

*For
Lizie*

# BOTTICELLI

*A Biography by* ELIZABETH RIPLEY

**J. B. LIPPINCOTT COMPANY** *Philadelphia   New York*

## ACKNOWLEDGEMENTS

I wish to thank Elizabeth Ourusoff for her encouragement and advice, and the Phaidon Press Ltd. for permitting me to reproduce a photograph of Botticelli's drawing for Dante's *Paradiso*.

The translations of quotations from Savonarola are taken from the biography of Girolamo Savonarola by Roberto Ridolphi.

# ILLUSTRATIONS

*Facing page*

ALESSANDRO Filipepi looked forward to his walk home from school, for there were many beautiful buildings in Florence. When he passed the new palace of the banker, Cosimo de Medici, he tried to imagine the rooms filled with paintings. Some day, he thought, he would become a painter and the Medici family would invite him to sit at their banquet table with Italy's best artists. He circled a low eight-sided building in the cathedral square, marveling at the pictures carved on the shining bronze doors. He walked by Santa Maria Maggiore wondering if ever he would be asked to paint a picture for this church.

Suddenly Sandro realized that he had reached the church of Ognissanti next to his home. He found his father in his workshop dipping hides in a vat of brown liquid. Mariano Filipepi looked at tall sturdy Sandro standing in the doorway. He could hardly believe that his youngest son was once a frail little boy who dreamed away his time at school. Sandro was now fourteen years old and ready to start work. His brother Simone, one year older, had a job in a bank in Naples, and another brother was a goldsmith. Mariano's oldest son, round and fat like a barrel, owned a leather shop in Florence. His friends nicknamed him "little cask," or Botticello, and because his youngest brother was often with him, they called little Sandro, Botticelli.

Sandro was delighted when his father decided he should work in the studio of the popular painter, Fra Filippo Lippi. The genial master taught Sandro to draw the human figure, grind paints and mix colors. Soon the boy was able to paint parts of his master's pictures.

Sandro worked in Fra Filippo's studio for eleven years. Then in 1469 he set up a workshop in his father's house. He was twenty-five years old.

Botticelli painted pictures for merchants' palaces, and long narrow panels to decorate their furniture. One panel showed "The Adoration of the Kings." Copying the composition of older artists, he placed the Virgin Mary and the Christ Child on the right end of the picture, arranging the long procession so skillfully that the small panel did not look crowded.

## ADORATION OF THE MAGI

Botticelli loved to visit Antonio Pollaiuolo's workshop where he admired the paintings of powerful nude figures which were now so popular in Florence. Antonio and his brother Piero spent hours dissecting corpses in order to find out how the human body was constructed. When the government of Florence decided to decorate their Council Hall with pictures of the seven virtues, they chose Piero to do the job. Other artists would be appointed to help him, Piero explained to Botticelli. Sandro wondered who these other artists would be.

A few days later a messenger called at Sandro's studio with a letter from the governors of Florence. Alessandro Botticelli had been chosen to paint one of the seven virtues, Fortitude, for the Council Hall. He hired a model whose majestic figure and dreamy expression attracted him. He watched her as she rose from her chair. In his picture he would try to show the graceful movement of her body under the long red robe which covered her knees.

The panels of the seven virtues were set up in the Council Hall one day in 1470. Florence's new ruler, Lorenzo de Medici came to see the pictures. The twenty-two-year-old grandson of Cosimo de Medici was a brilliant statesman, poet and scholar. He was far from handsome. His big nose was wide and flat, his skin dark, and his eyes small, but the people of Florence worshiped their charming new ruler who entertained them with tournaments and pageants, who danced with them in the carnivals and who rode in processions on his gray thoroughbred. They called him "The Magnificent."

Lorenzo stood for some time in the Council Hall, examining the paintings behind the judge's bench. Six of the seven virtues, carefully painted in bright colors, looked stiff and lifeless. Only one, Fortitude, seemed alive. This figure with a long torso and short legs was about to rise from her chair and step from the narrow panel. The artist who painted Fortitude would some day be a famous painter, Lorenzo decided as he left the Council Hall.

**FORTITUDE**

UFFIZI, FLORENCE

*Photo Alinari*

Lorenzo de Medici did not forget the name of Sandro Botticelli. He spoke of him to art lovers who wanted to buy pictures. One of them visited Sandro's workshop hoping to find a painting to give to Lorenzo's sister. He admired some Madonnas, passed on to a picture of an Adoration, and then paused for a long time in front of a painting of two women walking on the brow of a hill. Sandro told his visitor that it was a scene from the Bible story of Judith and Holofernes. Many other artists had painted the story of Judith and how she saved her city from destruction. This beautiful Jewish widow stole into the enemy camp one night and cut off the head of the sleeping general Holofernes. Then she returned across hill country to her home, followed by her servant girl who carried the general's head on a platter.

It was hard to believe that the beautiful blond girl in Botticelli's painting had just cut off a general's head. She was dressed in the style of Florentine women of Botticelli's day. Pearls were wound into her wavy hair and decorated the bodice of her light blue dress. She held a sword in her right hand and in her left the olive branch of peace. A coarse-faced servant girl in a yellow dress walked behind, carrying Holofernes' head. In the valley below, armed horsemen and foot soldiers were pouring out of the gate of a fortified town in pursuit of the fleeing enemy.

Botticelli's visitor was charmed by the lovely Judith who walked so lightly over the hillside, the folds of her dress billowing behind her. This painting, so different from others he had seen, he would present to Lorenzo's sister.

## JUDITH WITH THE HEAD OF HOLOFERNES

UFFIZI, FLORENCE

*Photo Alinari*

One day in 1472, the treasurer of Florence's guild of painters entered Botticelli's name in his account book, for on that day Sandro became a member of the Order of Saint Luke. He soon made friends with some of Italy's best-known painters. One new member, a handsome young man with blond wavy hair introduced himself to Botticelli. He had often admired Sandro's Madonnas and wanted to visit his studio. Sandro was impressed by this twenty-year-old artist who talked so intelligently about many subjects. Not only was he a talented painter, he was a fine singer, excellent horseman and an inventor. He told Sandro about the gigantic wings he was building which would make it possible for men to fly. His name was Leonardo da Vinci.

Leonardo called at Botticelli's workshop where Sandro was working on a painting of a Madonna and Child. He watched silently while Botticelli dipped a fine brush in thin color and painted the transparent veil which framed the Madonna's face. Leonardo was fascinated by the Madonna's sad expression. Perhaps she was already thinking of the death which awaited her son. Her long delicate fingers plucked a spear of grain from the bowl of grapes and wheat which a curly-headed angel offered her, while the Christ Child raised his hand in blessing.

Leonardo studied the landscape seen through the window in the background. It was a familiar scene. He had sketched the hills and winding river of the Arno valley many times. Botticelli turned to his young friend. It was not necessary to spend much time on painting a landscape he told Leonardo. Just try throwing a sponge against a wall, he said, and see what a beautiful landscape will appear in the spot it leaves.

Leonardo never followed the older painter's advice, but many years later the great Leonardo da Vinci quoted "our Botticelli" in his book on painting.

**MADONNA AND CHILD OF THE EUCHARIST**

ISABELLA STEWART GARDNER MUSEUM, BOSTON

The people of Florence were proud of their many beautiful churches. Prosperous merchants commissioned artists to paint Madonnas and Adorations to hang over altars and ordered pictures to decorate the walls. Many people talked of Pollaiuolo's powerful picture of the martyrdom of Saint Sebastian. They marveled at the violent action in the figures of the archers who aimed their arrows at the saint. Saint Sebastian, protector from the plague, was a favorite saint in Florence. Many artists had told the story of how the young Roman soldier was killed by archers, because he was a Christian. It was this story which Lorenzo asked Botticelli to paint for the Church of Santa Maria Maggiore.

Sandro put aside his paintings of Madonnas and started to work on his first commission for Lorenzo. He made pencil studies of nudes showing the construction of the human body, then he drew the figure of the saint on a tall narrow panel. The handsome young man, pierced with arrows almost filled the space. In the distance he drew in the archers who, having finished their job, were riding away in the distance. The executioners, the most important figures in Pollaiuolo's picture, were hardly visible. The martyred saint stood alone, his form sharply outlined against a clear sky. His face was sad but peaceful.

Botticelli painted the picture in soft clear colors and when it was finished it was hung on a pillar of the Church of Santa Maria Maggiore on Saint Sebastian's feast day. Lorenzo de Medici was moved by its quiet melancholy. He gazed for a long time at the youth's face framed by a halo of dark curly hair, for it reminded him so much of his beloved brother, handsome Giuliano.

SAINT SEBASTIAN

STAATLICHE MUSEUM, BERLIN

Giuliano de Medici, dressed in shining armor and a cape sewn with pearls and rubies, rode into the square of Santa Croce. The crowds cheered madly. Ahead of him rode a standard bearer carrying Giuliano's pennant designed by the Medici's favorite artist, Botticelli. On a bright blue background Sandro had painted Pallas, goddess of war, standing on burning olive branches. Behind her was the rising sun.

Giuliano smiled up at beautiful blond Simonetta who watched her lover from a balcony. The tournament in honor of Simonetta Vespucci was about to begin.

Giuliano broke the lances of many armed knights that January day in 1475. As each rider fell the people went wild with joy for they adored Lorenzo's handsome daredevil brother. Poems were written and songs sung about Giuliano and his lovely lady Simonetta. Lorenzo's favorite poet, Politian, brilliant Greek and Roman scholar, compared him to the God of War. In a long poem he described how Mars, having taken off his armor lay dreaming of his lady, while Cupid whispered in his ear that she would lead him to victory.

This was the story Botticelli painted on a chest which Lorenzo ordered for his palace. On the right of the long narrow panel lay the god of war and on the left his lady wearing Roman dress. Behind, three children, half goat, half human, played with the war god's lance. One of these wore his helmet and another blew on a horn which he held to the sleeping god's ear. A fourth, wearing an armored breastplate, was crawling on the ground.

**MARS AND VENUS**

Thirty-three-year-old Botticelli was becoming the most popular painter in Florence. Wealthy Giovanni Lami, banker for the Medici, commissioned him to paint an Adoration of the Kings for one of Florence's biggest churches. Hoping to impress Lorenzo, he instructed Sandro to show portraits of the Medici and their friends in his picture.

Botticelli did not arrange the worshipers in a long procession as he had done some years before. Instead he grouped them on either side of the Holy Family which he placed in the center of the picture. A white-haired king in a dark cloak embroidered in gold, knelt before the Virgin, reaching toward the Child's feet which he was about to kiss. His strong sharp profile was that of Cosimo de Medici, grandfather of Lorenzo. A dark-haired king in a red robe lined with ermine knelt in the center. His profile was weaker than the older king's. It was the face of Cosimo's oldest son Piero, father of Lorenzo.

In the left corner stood a haughty young man in a crimson doublet, hands crossed on his sword. The head of one of Lorenzo's favorite horses nestled against his shoulder. This proud man who seemed to be lost in thought was Botticelli's idea of Lorenzo.

A man with dark curly hair, wearing a black cloak, stood in the group on the right. His eyes were downcast, his expression sullen. His features were those of dashing Giuliano.

Some of the worshipers gazed in adoration at the Holy Family, others looked straight ahead. One blond man looked out of the picture. The forefinger of his hand grasping his light blue cloak pointed to himself to show that he, Giovanni Lami, was the donor of the painting.

Botticelli did not sign his canvas, but in the right-hand corner he painted a tall man in a gold-colored cloak who gazed out of the picture as if he were trying to attract attention to himself; "I, Botticelli," he seemed to say, "painted this picture of the Adoration."

## ADORATION OF THE MAGI

UFFIZI, FLORENCE

*Photo Alinari*

When the last coat of varnish had dried, Botticelli's Adoration was placed in an ornate gold frame and carried to the Church of Santa Maria Novella where it was hung over the carved marble altar in the Lami family chapel. The people of Florence came to marvel at the picture. Among the worshipers they recognized familiar faces, the great Cosimo, his son Piero, Lorenzo and the adored Giuliano. They recognized other faces too—well-known bankers and merchants dressed in rich robes, and the artist Botticelli whom they had seen many times riding through the streets of Florence on his way to the Medici palace.

"Sandro lives at home," his father wrote in his income tax return for 1477, "and works when he chooses." But Botticelli's studio was a busy one. His pupils copied pictures of his sweet-faced Madonnas, which were sold in his workshop. Filipino Lippi, son of his old teacher sometimes helped him on his big commissions. There were orders for Adorations, Madonnas and curly-headed angels, and Lorenzo often called on him to paint pictures illustrating Greek and Roman myths.

**SELF PORTRAIT. Detail from ADORATION OF THE MAGI**

UFFIZI, FLORENCE

*Photo Alinari*

Botticelli loved to listen to the conversation at Lorenzo's banquet table. Witty, hook-nosed Politian, ten years younger than Sandro chose his words cleverly, quoting frequently from Greek and Latin writers. Sandro, who knew no Greek or Latin, often read Politian's Italian poems which brought the ancient gods and goddesses to life. Over and over he read the poem which pictured Venus walking "in a perpetual garden," shaded by a tree with golden fruit.

"Around me were violets and lilies in the green grass, and pretty new flowers, blue, green, yellow, white and red." Here too was Flora, goddess of spring "holding up her apron full of flowers." It was this scene which Botticelli painted for one of Lorenzo's cousins.

Venus, goddess of love, stood in an orange grove carpeted with spring blossoms like the ones that covered the hillsides around Florence, City of Flowers. Flora walked lightly over the bright carpet strewing blossoms from the skirt of her flowered dress. A nymph in a filmy veil was fleeing from a wind god who embraced her. His icy breath had broken the blossom which she held in her mouth. On the left of the picture stood the god Mercury breaking up a tiny cloud with his magic staff. A Cupid, floating in the trees above, aimed his arrow at three dancing nymphs.

**PRIMAVERA (SPRING)**

UFFIZI, FLORENCE

*Photo Alinari*

When Sandro painted the three blond willowy graces he must have thought of Giuliano's beautiful lady, Simonetta, who had died only one year after the tournament fought in her honor. The people of Florence were saddened by the loss and mourned for grief-stricken Giuliano.

There were some people who hated Giuliano and his brother. The banker, Francesco Pazzi, jealous of the Medici, plotted to overthrow them. On a Sunday morning in April, 1478, crowds worshiped at the cathedral. Lorenzo and his brother stood before the altar. Behind them stood Francesco Pazzi. The solemn moment of the Mass was about to begin. The priest lifted the host, a bell tinkled, the brothers knelt. Pazzi lunged forward sinking his knife into Giuliano's neck. A hired assassin struck him again. Giuliano, covered with blood, fell dead on the altar steps. As two armed assassins attacked him, Lorenzo drew his sword and ran to the back of the church. The doors of the sacristy slammed behind him. In vain the assassins tried to force themselves into the little room. Lorenzo, his cloak wrapped about his wounded arm waited to be rescued.

Outside crowds swarmed into the streets crying, "The Medici have been murdered!" drowning out cries of Pazzi followers who shouted, "Freedom!"

A furious mob dragged Francesco to the government palace, tied a rope around his neck and threw him out of the window. One after the other the assassins were flung from the palace windows, where they dangled before the angry crowd. Friends carried Giuliano's bleeding body to his home. People shouted "Palle!" war cry of the Medici. The Pazzi conspiracy had failed.

The next morning the assassins' corpses had been removed, but the people of Florence watched fascinated as a tall, light-haired artist painted more than life size pictures of the hanging bodies on the palace wall. Botticelli, painter of Madonnas, nymphs and angels, had been commissioned by the government to perform this gruesome task, a warning to those who tried to overthrow their rulers.

**THREE GRACES**
**Detail from PRIMAVERA**

UFFIZI, FLORENCE

*Photo Alinari*

Lorenzo, miraculously spared, was now more popular than ever, while his enemies became violent in their hatred. One of the fiercest was the Pope who ordered Botticelli's pictures of assassins erased from the government palace walls. Then came news that Pope Sixtus had persuaded the king of Naples to start a war against the Medici. Soon the king's army and the papal troops were marching north toward Florence. The people, loyal to Lorenzo, fought valiantly, but the city was encircled. The siege lasted for two years. The citizens, tired and hungry, began to grumble. Lorenzo, fearing that they might turn against him, decided on a daring plan.

No one recognized the horsemen who galloped out of the city one gray December morning, holding their cloaks before their faces. The gates of Florence closed behind them. One rider dug his spurs into the sides of his gray thoroughbred. Lorenzo was on his way to Naples. He stopped in Pisa and wrote a letter to the governors of Florence. He would try to make peace with the king of Naples, he wrote, in order to save his city from destruction.

Through that winter Florentines waited anxiously. Then came news that the king of Naples had agreed to end the war. The people went wild with joy. One sunny April day in 1480 Lorenzo rode triumphantly into the city. As he clattered through the streets, citizens strewed his path with flowers.

A few days later Sandro visited the Medici palace to discuss a painting which would celebrate this glorious peace.

Botticelli's picture showed the Medicis' goddess, Pallas, wearing a dress trimmed with olive branches and the three ring insignia of Lorenzo's family. She held a lance in her left hand and with her right she grasped the thick locks of a cringing centaur. In this way Botticelli symbolized Lorenzo's triumph over his enemy. In the background was a ship sailing into the bay of Naples, the ship which had brought Lorenzo back to Florence.

**PALLAS AND THE CENTAUR**

UFFIZI, FLORENCE

*Photo Alinari*

From his studio window Botticelli could see the cemetery of the Church of Ognissanti, the church which he passed every time he went to the Medici palace. Sometimes he stopped inside to look at the pictures which Ghirlandajo was painting on one of the walls. He could not help admiring the carefully drawn figures and realistically painted landscapes. Ghirlandajo, five years younger than Sandro, was one of the most popular fresco painters in Florence. He filled his pictures with portraits of important bankers and merchants and familiar scenes of Florence, but Botticelli thought his figures looked stiff. He knew he could put life into Ghirlandajo's figure of the Madonna and movement into the lines of her drapery.

A few years after Ghirlandajo had finished his fresco in the Church of Ognissanti, he was asked to paint another fresco in the same church—a picture of Saint Jerome in his study— to fill the space on the left of a doorway. On the right would be Saint Augustine, to be painted by Sandro Botticelli.

A contract was signed and the artists started to work. Day after day they painted in the cool silent church. Other artists who came to watch were impressed by the vigor of Botticelli's picture. Saint Augustine sat at his desk, pen in hand, lost in a trance. Because Sandro showed the figure as if seen from below, the saint looked almost monumental. This moving picture of Saint Augustine, made Ghirlandajo's Saint Jerome look wooden.

Visitors from many cities came to look at the paintings. Travelers returning to Rome talked about Sandro Botticelli's latest picture. Pope Sixtus wondered about this artist, whose pictures of assassins he had ordered erased. Should he call him to Rome to decorate his new private chapel? He had already decided to commission Ghirlandajo to paint frescoes on one of the walls. He admired the serene pictures of young Perugino and the realistic frescoes of Cosimo Roselli. He would invite these artists to decorate the other walls. Then, one day in 1481, Sixtus IV sent a letter to Botticelli.

**SAINT AUGUSTINE**

CHURCH OF OGNISSANTI, FLORENCE

*Photo Alinari*

Four Florentine painters rode into Rome in January of 1481. As they clattered through the shabby streets filled with beggars, they thought of the shining palaces and beautiful churches of their own city.

The Pope received the artists in his narrow vaulted chapel under a blue ceiling dotted with gold stars. He pointed to the bare side walls under the arched windows. He wanted the artists to cover these walls with one continuous band of pictures. On one wall would be scenes from the life of Moses, on the other the life of Christ. Between the windows would be portraits of thirty-two Popes. Each artist was assigned spaces to fill and subjects to paint.

On the right wall, facing the Pope's throne, Botticelli was to picture Christ's Temptation. Sixtus told Sandro what he wanted him to paint. He reminded the artist to show the splendid new hospital which he had built in Rome, and portraits of the Pope's family, especially his favorite nephew. Somewhere in the painting he must picture the religious ceremony called "The Purification of the Leper," which symbolized the cleansing of Christ's soul. In this ceremony a priest would be sprinkling a leper with bird's blood. Where, Botticelli wondered, would he have room to tell the story of Christ's temptation?

A scaffolding was built and the artists started to work. Sixtus visited the chapel often, and was pleased that Botticelli had placed the hospital of San Spirito in the center of his picture. In front was an altar where the ceremony took place. A priest accepted a basin of blood from an altar boy. A lovely woman carrying a bundle of faggots hurried forward, her drapery billowing around her. The leper, his hand on his heart stood on the altar steps. On either side Sixtus recognized members of his family who paid little attention to the ceremony. He hardly noticed that on a rocky peak in the background Christ talked to a monk whose claw feet and bat wings showed him to be the Devil. From the top of Sixtus' hospital, Satan tempted Christ again, while on the right, Jesus pushed the Devil from a cliff.

## PURIFICATION OF THE LEPER

SISTINE CHAPEL, ROME

*Photo Anderson*

While Sandro was working on the picture of Christ's temptation, his assistants were painting another picture on the opposite wall. Botticelli often climbed the scaffolding to direct the work. In the lower right corner an assistant was transferring a portion of Sandro's drawing to the plaster wall. The scene showed Moses killing an Egyptian, while in the background, Moses, fearful of what he had done, was fleeing from the scene.

Botticelli moved to another part of the picture where an assistant was painting Moses driving a group of shepherds from a well where two shepherdesses were standing with their sheep. Botticelli picked up a brush and started to work on the women's figures, bringing grace into the poses and movement into the drapery. Soon these blond shepherdesses looked like the beautiful graces in Sandro's painting of Spring.

While an assistant painted the figure of Moses watering the maidens' flocks, Botticelli examined the upper part of the picture where a pupil was drawing the outline of a hillside, the hillside where God appeared in a burning bush saying to Moses:

"Put off thy shoes from off thy feet, for the place where on thou standest is holy ground."

Copying Botticelli's drawing the pupil had shown Moses taking off his shoes, and at the top of the hill, kneeling before God who was telling him to free his people from captivity.

The last scene in Sandro's drawing showed Moses leading his people from Egypt. An assistant handed Botticelli a brush. For some time he worked on the figures of the men and women who followed Moses. There were young men with long hair, bearded men in turbans, women carrying bundles on their heads, and a boy with wavy blond hair carrying a fox terrier.

All through the spring and summer the artists and their assistants painted in Sixtus' chapel. Botticelli's pupils started another picture of Moses punishing the leaders of a rebellion. This story, Sixtus believed, was a warning to those who would disobey the Pope. Botticelli, who took little interest in the subject told his assistants to finish the work. He was tired of hot noisy Rome and homesick for Florence, but he had not started to paint the portraits of the Popes.

## SCENES FROM THE LIFE OF MOSES

**SISTINE CHAPEL, ROME**

*Photo Anderson*

Botticelli painted the figures of seven Popes, outlining them with dark shadows so that they stood out of their niches like pieces of sculpture. Then in October he left for Florence.

The City of Flowers was gayer than ever. The war with the Pope had been forgotten. Once more Lorenzo staged tournaments and carnivals. Artists were busy turning out paintings for prosperous clients.

In Lorenzo's library Botticelli was shown a book which had just been printed by a new machine called a printing press. He had often read this book by Dante in a handsome hand-lettered volume belonging to Lorenzo. Now he turned the printed pages of *The Divine Comedy* slowly, studying each illustration, for these pictures were prints of drawings he had made before he left for Rome. The prints were disappointing, Botticelli thought. Some day he would make new illustrations for the book. But first he must fill orders for paintings of Madonnas.

A panel, four feet square, stood on an easel in his studio. It showed a Madonna surrounded by angels which were gracefully fitted in a circle, a shape which had become popular in Florence. Botticelli had painted many of these tondos. Some had to be changed to suit the wishes of the client who wanted to add an angel here, or change a pose there. Many did not satisfy Botticelli, but he knew that this tondo was one of the most beautiful he had painted.

The lines of the Madonna's pose and that of the angels followed the curve of the circle. In the center was the Child's head. Two angels held a delicate gold crown above the Virgin. In her left hand was a pomegranate, and in her right she held a pen which she dipped into the inkwell held by an angel. The Child, looking toward heaven, guided her hand as she wrote the song of the Virgin Mary in the book beside her. This Latin chant, called the Magnificat, was clearly written on the pages. A distant landscape let air and light into the picture.

The Madonna of the Magnificat was Botticelli's glorious tribute to the Virgin Mary.

**MADONNA OF THE MAGNIFICAT**

UFFIZI, FLORENCE

*Photo Alinari*

Almost every day clients called at Botticelli's workshop to order paintings of Madonnas. His pupils were busy turning out pictures which looked like Botticelli's and which were sold as soon as they were finished. One day a customer admired a sweet-faced Madonna surrounded by angels and told the pupil who had painted it he would return the next day to buy it. That evening, after the pupil had left the workshop, Sandro cut out red paper caps and pasted them on the angels' heads. The next morning, the pupil, speechless with surprise, waited for the customer to arrive; but he was even more amazed when the customer did not even notice that the angels in the picture were wearing the caps of Florentine judges. While the dumfounded youth accompanied the client to his house to collect his money, Sandro, delighted that he had fooled a stupid customer, tore off the caps before his assistant returned.

When Botticelli became weary of painting Madonnas and angels, he loved to ride out to Lorenzo's country palace in Careggi, where people talked of pagan gods and goddesses and of ancient myths of Greece and Rome. He never tired of hearing Politian recite his poem about the birth of Venus:

> "A maiden not a human face I saw
>   By wanton Zephyrs drifted to the shore
>   Upon a cockle shell."

What a beautiful picture this would make! Sandro could see the goddess of love, or was it Simonetta, nude except for the long yellow hair falling about her shoulders, gliding across the sea in a pearly shell. A wind god and goddess would be blowing her toward the shore where the figure of Spring was holding a rose cloak embroidered with daisies in which to wrap the lovely goddess. Refreshed by the thought of this picture, Botticelli returned to his studio and started to paint.

Politian often saw the painting he had inspired, for as soon as the Birth of Venus was finished Lorenzo bought it for his palace.

**BIRTH OF VENUS**

UFFIZI, FLORENCE

*Photo Alinari*

Visitors to Botticelli's studio were haunted by the lovely face of Venus. They saw the same melancholy face again in a huge altarpiece which stood in another part of his workshop. Sandro had started this picture as soon as he returned from Rome. The beautiful Virgin sitting enthroned, holding her baby on her lap, wore the same sad expression as Botticelli's goddess of love. But there were no pagan gods or nymphs in this painting. On either side of the Virgin's throne were Christian saints. On the left Saint Catherine robed in green, Saint Ambrose dressed as an archbishop, absorbed in the book he was reading and Saint Barnabas in red, whose lined face and sad eyes betrayed his deep emotion. On the right stood Saint John the Baptist holding a cross, his young face drawn in pain. Beside him was winged Saint Michael in shining armor, and behind, Saint Augustine, head bowed in contemplation.

Two angels pulled aside a red curtain lined with ermine revealing the Madonna on her throne. Two more angels held Christ's crown of thorns and the nails which had fastened him to the cross.

Inscribed on a marble plaque at the foot of the Virgin's throne was a line from Dante's *Divine Comedy*. Quoting from his favorite book, Botticelli had written in Italian:

"Virgin Mother, Daughter of Thy Son."

# MADONNA ENTHRONED WITH SIX SAINTS

## Saint Barnabas Altarpiece

UFFIZI, FLORENCE

*Photo Alinari*

Botticelli painted a set of little panels as a border for the base of his altarpiece. This border, or predella, showed stories from the lives of saints. One pictured the vision of Saint Augustine.

This saintly bishop, writer of religious books, was walking along the beach one day pondering on the meaning of the Holy Trinity, when suddenly he came upon a little boy digging a hole in the sand. The bishop watched him silently. The boy ran to the shore, filled his spoon with water and emptied it into the hole. Back and forth he ran with spoonful after spoonful of water. He wanted to put all the sea into the hole, he told the bishop. Saint Augustine, surprised, asked if this could be done. The boy looked up at the kindly bishop. He would rather do this, he replied, than try to explain the Holy Trinity which was far deeper and greater than the sea. Then he vanished from the beach.

VISION OF SAINT AUGUSTINE
**Detail of Predella of SAINT BARNABAS ALTARPIECE**

UFFIZI, FLORENCE

*Photo Alinari*

In the summer of 1486 Lorenzo de Medici planned a brilliant wedding for his cousin, Lorenzo Tornabuoni. The bride, Giovanna Albizzi, was, wrote one Florentine, "a lady of singular beauty." Botticelli had often talked to her at the Medici palace. He was impressed by her knowledge of Greek and Roman classics, and she admired his paintings of Spring and the Birth of Venus.

The newly married couple moved into the two-storied villa which had been built for them near Lorenzo's country palace. The walls of the little chapel were bright with frescoes by Ghirlandajo and one long room on the second floor was decorated with pictures by Botticelli. The bridegroom's father, wishing to please his daughter-in-law, had commissioned her favorite painter to cover the walls with pictures of Giovanna and her husband.

One wall glorified the bride. Beautiful Giovanna welcomed four lovely graces to her court. One of these goddesses was dropping a flower into the napkin which Giovanna was holding.

Long after Giovanna's death, someone covered Botticelli's pictures with layers of white paint. Many years later, the layers were removed. Today parts of the picture have disappeared, but the graceful figures in light flowing drapery remain.

## GIOVANNA WITH VENUS AND GRACES

**LOUVRE, PARIS**

*Frescoes from Villa Lemmi*

Facing the painting of Giovanna and the graces, was a picture of her husband. Lorenzo Tornabuoni, dressed in the long gown and red skull cap of a Florentine scholar, was being introduced to the court of the Queen of Philosophy. The queen, wearing a fur-trimmed robe, sat on a throne surrounded by six maidens who represented learning. On her left were Dialectic, Rhetoric and Arithmetic, and on her right, Music, Geometry and Astrology. A maiden in a red cloak was leading the bridegroom into the court. In this way Botticelli showed that Lorenzo Tornabuoni, like his cousin Lorenzo de Medici, was a patron of art and learning.

## LORENZO TORNABUONI AND THE LIBERAL ARTS

LOUVRE, PARIS

*Frescoes from Villa Lemmi*

Sandro was delighted when his brother Simone gave up his job in Naples and returned to his father's home. The brothers often talked until late at night about books and painting. Simone was proud of his younger brother's success, and admired Sandro's Madonnas and Adorations which decorated many of Florence's churches. He was especially moved by the tondo Madonna which Sandro was painting in his studio. He was haunted by the Virgin's sad sweet face and the dreamy expression of the Child who rested His hand on a pomegranate.

When the painting was finished Sandro placed it in the frame he had designed which was decorated with gold foliage on a deep blue ground. This was one of Sandro's finest paintings, Simone thought. The Madonna looked like the Venus Botticelli had painted for Lorenzo, but sadder and more beautiful.

Simone often spoke to his brother about a monk named Savonarola who was preaching fiery sermons at the convent of San Marco. Every Sunday the Friar hurled terrifying warnings from the pulpit. Florence would be destroyed, he thundered, unless the people reformed their evil ways. He attacked the pleasure-loving citizens who thought only of carnivals and fancy clothes and the rulers of Florence who decorated their palaces with pictures of pagan gods and goddesses.

Botticelli, impressed by what his brother told him, was anxious to listen to one of the Friar's sermons. On a Sunday morning Sandro and Simone set off for the convent of San Marco.

## MADONNA OF THE POMEGRANATE

UFFIZI, FLORENCE

*Photo Alinari*

Botticelli recognized many familiar faces in the crowd which poured into the Church of San Marco. A young man with a crooked nose and rumpled clothes pushed his way through the door. Botticelli had seen the rough-mannered youth before. He was the talented sculptor whom Lorenzo had invited to live at the Medici palace. His name was Michelangelo.

A hush came over the murmuring crowd as a little man in a monk's cowl climbed into the pulpit. Botticelli was shocked by the ugly face which peered from the black hood. But as soon as the monk began to speak, Sandro forgot his curved nose, thick lips and dark leathery skin. He did not use the refined language of Politian, nor did he quote from Greek and Latin poetry. He spoke the language of the common people and quoted only from the Bible. The Day of Judgment would come soon, he cried, when the pleasure-seeking Florentines and their pagan-minded rulers would be punished for their sins. The fiery monk, like the prophets in the Bible, brought a message of warning to his people. Botticelli was deeply moved.

Savonarola's resounding words rang in Sandro's ears when he returned to his studio. He hardly noticed the unfinished painting of nymphs and goddesses which stood on an easel. He picked up a brush and started to work on an altarpiece for one of Florence's new churches. The big canvas told the story of the Annunciation. Phrases from the Bible ran through his mind as he painted the familiar scene of an angel appearing before the Virgin:

"And the angel said unto her, Fear not . . . thou shalt . . . bring forth a son, and shalt call his name Jesus."

Botticelli showed the angel at the moment he appeared before the Virgin, the folds of his red robe floating behind him, as if he had just alighted. The Virgin, interrupted in her reading, reached out in a gesture of surprise. An open window in the background framed a peaceful landscape, and reverent silence seemed to fill the room.

## THE ANNUNCIATION

UFFIZI, FLORENCE

*Photo Alinari*

During the spring of 1490 Sandro and Simone listened to Savonarola's Lenten sermons. They heard him attack the wealthy merchants of Florence and artists who painted pictures for their palaces.

"Not a merchant can order a wedding but his daughter must bestow her furbelows in a chest painted with heathen fables," the Friar cried. "What shall I say of you, ye painters who expose half-naked figures to the public view?"

Was Savonarola thinking of the panel of Mars and Venus, which Botticelli had painted for the Medici? Sandro could not forget the Friar's words when he started to work on a marriage chest he had just been commissioned to decorate. Instead of a "heathen fable," he chose a Bible story. On separate panels he painted scenes from the life of Esther. Sandro had often read the story of the Jewish girl who was married to a Persian king. When Esther's father, Mordecai, refused to bow before his daughter's husband, the king ordered that every Jew in the land be put to death. Then Mordecai "rent his clothes . . . and came even before the king's gate."

This was the scene Botticelli painted on one of the panels of the marriage chest. Mordecai, head plunged in his hands, sat outside the palace gate. His torn clothing was scattered on the steps in front of him. There were no graceful decorations, no landscape views to relieve the bare wall behind him. This stark scene, shown in a cold hard light expressed the tragedy of that moment.

# THE DERELICT

**COLLECTION PRINCIPE PALLAVICINI, ROME**

*Photo Anderson*

At the time Savonarola was preaching at San Marco, Botticelli, commissioned by Florence's guild of goldsmiths, painted an altarpiece for one of San Marco's chapels. When the picture was placed above the altar it seemed to bring light into the dark church. People who came to hear the Friar gazed with wonder at the brilliant panel. The figures of four saints filled the lower half of the picture. Saint John the Evangelist, holding a book, raised his hand toward heaven. Saint Augustine, in bishop's robes, was writing in a book. Saint Jerome, in the scarlet robes of a cardinal, looked upwards, his hand against his heart. Another bishop, Saint Eligius, patron saint of goldsmiths, raised his hand in blessing. Botticelli's pupils had helped him paint these austere figures posed against a barren landscape, and the figures of God and the Virgin seated on a bank of clouds; but Botticelli himself had painted the circle of angels dancing in the gold sky above.

When San Marco could no longer hold the throng which came to hear the Friar, Savonarola preached in the cathedral. Sometimes Lorenzo came to listen. When friends of the Medici urged the Friar to stop his attacks on Florence's popular ruler, Savonarola replied that Lorenzo was the city's foremost citizen. "But," he continued, "I shall remain, and he will pass away."

A few months later Lorenzo became seriously ill. In the spring of 1492 he was carried to his villa in Careggi. One day while Politian watched by the bedside of his dying friend, Lorenzo asked him to send for Savonarola.

"Send me the one honest friar I know," he whispered.

When Savonarola arrived at Careggi, Lorenzo was too weak to speak. The Friar looked at the man whose death he had predicted. "God is good," was all he said.

Lorenzo lifted his head to kiss the crucifix which was held before him and fell back dead.

**CORONATION OF THE VIRGIN**

UFFIZI, FLORENCE

*Photo Alinari*

Lorenzo's son, Piero, became the new ruler of Florence. He was strong and handsome; he loved to ride and hunt, but he did not inherit his father's brilliant mind. He took no interest in books or painting. Poets and artists were no longer invited to the Medici palace, and Botticelli received few commissions.

In the spring of 1494 Sandro and Simone bought a house and vineyard on a hillside outside Florence. From the tower of their villa they looked over an olive grove to the winding Arno River. In this peaceful home Sandro had time to paint and read. He studied books on painting. He was impressed by a description of a famous picture by the Greek artist Apelles. So clearly did the author describe every detail of this picture "Calumny," that Botticelli was able to see it vividly in his mind.

On a small canvas Botticelli painted the picture of Calumny as he saw it. A judge sat on a throne, while Ignorance and Suspicion whispered in his long ears. Envy, a bearded man wearing a dark hood, pointed at the judge. A woman in flowing robes, representing Calumny, dragged a young man, Innocence, by the hair. Two graceful women, Fraud and Treachery, twined roses in Calumny's blond locks. Remorse, a hag in black, looked back at naked Truth who pointed toward heaven. The columns in the background were decorated with scenes from the Bible and from Greek myths. Beyond the arches was a clear blue sky and sea. Sandro did not try to sell this disturbing picture. When it was finished he gave it to a friend.

From time to time Sandro rode into Florence to supervise his workshop and to listen to Savonarola's sermons. The Friar's prophecies made a deep impression on Sandro and Simone. A foreign power would come soon, Savonarola thundered, to punish Florence for its sins.

In the fall of 1494, the king of France led his army over the mountains into Italy. As the French marched toward Florence, Piero did nothing to defend the city. Indignant citizens rose up against their ruler. In terror Piero fled. A few days later Charles VIII rode into Florence. Another of Savonarola's prophecies had come true.

**CALUMNY**

UFFIZI, FLORENCE

*Photo Alinari*

The people of Florence were not impressed by the deformed little French king, and they were not sorry when, a few days later, he led his army south toward Rome. Florence was without a ruler, so the city council turned to Savonarola.

"You know I have never wanted to intervene in affairs of state," the Friar replied. "Do you think I would do so now if I did not see that it was necessary for the health of your souls?" Then he outlined a constitution which the city council adopted.

But reform in government was not enough, Savonarola thundered from the pulpit. The people must reform their souls. Games and carnivals were forbidden. Gamblers were arrested and women wearing low-necked dresses were put in prison. The City of Flowers was no longer gay. Many of Botticelli's friends had left Florence. Leonardo was in Milan, Politian had died, Lorenzo Tornabuoni had been executed by the Savonarola government. Only one Medici patron remained in the city. This was another Lorenzo, who had once commissioned Botticelli to illustrate Dante's *Divine Comedy*. Sandro, who had never liked the drawings, welcomed the chance to make new ones.

Using smooth sheets of parchment and a silver-point pencil he started to draw pictures of Dante's journey into hell. Here and there he strengthened the delicate lines with touches of black ink. He showed how Dante, guided by the poet Virgil, descended from one circle of Inferno to the next. With each new circle the tortures of the damned became more terrible. On separate sheets Botticelli showed each circle exactly as it was described by Dante. Robbers, doomed to eternal fire, tried to ward off flames which poured down on them. Racketeers were fixed head-downwards in the sand while flames consumed their feet. In one of the lowest circles counterfeiters and forgers were tormented by diseases. Some scratched incessantly and others writhed in agony. When Dante stopped to talk to people he had known, Virgil pulled him downwards until they reached the lowest circle of Inferno.

**DANTE'S INFERNO**

**Drawing**

STAATLICHE MUSEUM, BERLIN

In the semidarkness of the lowest circle of Inferno, Dante saw towering shapes that looked like buildings.

"What city is this?" he asked his guide, and Virgil answered that these were not towers but chained giants whose legs were fixed forever in a well because they had once revolted against the gods.

One giant, Anteas, who was not bound, reached out a mammoth hand, picked up the poets and placed them lightly in the lowest hole of hell. In the center of this circle, where traitors were frozen in a sea of ice, Dante saw hairy three-faced Satan who was chewing a sinner in each mouth. This was the last step of the poets journey into hell. Virgil and Dante started their upward climb,

> "... he first and I second
> until I saw, through a round opening
> the beautiful things that heaven bears,
> and came forth again to see the stars."

**DANTE'S INFERNO**

**The Fettered Giants. Drawing**

STAATLICHE MUSEUM, BERLIN

Savonarola continued to hurl terrifying warnings from the pulpit. Over and over he attacked pleasure-loving citizens who spent their money on fine furniture, expensive clothes and paintings of pagan subjects. His followers built a roaring bonfire in the public square, while boys went from house to house collecting furniture, clothing and pictures to feed the flames. In a frenzy of repentance people hurled books and paintings on the fire. Canvases of nude gods and goddesses blackened, curled up and disappeared forever.

Pictures should not be painted for people's pleasure, but for saving peoples souls. "Paint Hell and Paradise!" Savonarola cried. Botticelli thought of these words as he filled sheet after sheet of parchment with drawings for Dante's poem. He showed each step of the poets' ascent of Purgatory, where souls were cleansed of their sins before they entered heaven. The poets climbed from one ledge to the next until they reached the earthly Paradise. Here Virgil bade his friend goodbye, and Dante waited for his beloved Beatrice to descend from heaven and guide him up to Paradise.

Beatrice, whose death Dante had mourned on earth, descended from heaven in a rain of flowers. First Dante must confess his sins, she told him, before he could ascend to Paradise. Cleansed of his sins in a stream of holy water, he was ready to mount to heaven. Beatrice fixed her eyes on the sun and guided her lover upward.

Botticelli showed the soaring figures emerging from the treetops of the earthly-Paradise. Below them was the stream where Dante had been cleansed. Beatrice, the taller of the two, held Dante by the arm. Their faces were reflected faintly in the earth beneath. This unfinished drawing is one of the most beautiful of Sandro's illustrations for Dante's *Paradiso*.

DANTE'S PARADISO

**Drawing**

STAATLICHE MUSEUM, BERLIN

Beatrice and Dante soared from one sphere of heaven to the next until they reached the ninth circle, the highest sphere of heaven. Dante was dazzled by the brilliant point of light above him. Beatrice told him that the light came from God and around it revolved nine rings of singing angels.

Botticelli showed Dante shading his eyes from the blinding light, while Beatrice, pointing heavenward, described the nine orders of angels which revolved about it. Each order carried a different emblem and each was carefully labeled in the right-hand margin of the drawing. For the first time, Sandro decided to sign his drawing. Sandro Di Mariano (son of Mariano) he wrote in tiny letters on the card held by one of the angels in the lowest circle.

**DANTE'S PARADISO**

**The Ninth Sphere of Heaven. Drawing**

STAATLICHE MUSEUM, BERLIN

Botticelli's patron died before the drawings for Dante's poem were finished. Sandro put aside his silver-point pencil and sheets of parchment. From time to time he visited his workshop. But the noisy city tired him. He seldom went to hear the Friar's sermons, but Simone, returning from San Marco would bring him news of Florence.

Savonarola continued to preach reform. He attacked the wickedness of certain priests who lived in luxury instead of giving their money to the poor. From Rome came an angry letter from the Pope ordering Savonarola to stop preaching.

"Rome may do what she pleases," the Friar replied. "She will never put out this flame!" His resounding attacks continued and thousands flocked to hear him. Letter after letter the Pope sent to Savonarola, and each time the monk ignored the Holy Father's orders.

"You think, Rome, to frighten me, and I know no fear!" he cried.

In the spring of 1498 the Pope commanded the governors of Florence to arrest this Friar who disobeyed his orders. An angry mob broke into San Marco killing many monks. Savonarola was bound and led to the Government palace. Every day the monk's frail body was twisted on the rack until he confessed sins which the next day he denied. Many of his followers were arrested. People feared even to mention his name.

Then early one morning Savonarola was hanged and burned in the public square. His terror-striken followers watched silently as the wracked body of the Friar was consumed.

Botticelli was haunted by the Friar's martyrdom. When he filled commissions for religious pictures he showed tragic scenes from the lives of saints. For one of Savonarola's most ardent followers, he painted the death of Saint Jerome. This little panel showed the dying saint receiving the last communion. Two monks supported him tenderly as he knelt before a priest who offered him the wafer, symbol of Christ's body. His massive head, too big for his frail body, his open mouth, long nose and sunken eyes seemed to express the saint's suffering.

## THE LAST COMMUNION OF SAINT JEROME

COURTESY OF THE METROPOLITAN MUSEUM OF ART, NEW YORK

*Bequest of Benjamin Altman, 1913*

The spirit of Savonarola lived on for many years. People did not forget his warnings that Florence would be destroyed. As the year 1500 approached, many feared the end of the world. Some turned to the Bible for comfort, finding a message of hope in the story of the Apocalypse. In this strange book Saint John told how God showed him visions of the end of the world, and how, after the universe had been destroyed, he saw a new and shining world where people lived in happiness and peace.

Botticelli, pondering on the meaning of these visions, painted a picture of the birth of Christ. In the foreground three saints were welcomed into Paradise by angels carrying the olive branch of peace. In the background devils hid in the cracks between rocks. A path zigzagged up a grassy slope to the Holy Family and the manger. On either side of an angel of peace brought kings and shepherds to worship at the scene. In a light blue sky twelve angels, carrying crowns and olive branches, danced around a circle of golden light. The heavenly dance expressed the joy and hope which Christ's birth brought to mankind.

As Sandro painted his vision of the Birth of Christ, words from the Apocalypse ran through his mind. When the picture was finished he wrote a Greek inscription across the top.

"This picture, I, Alessandro, painted at the end of the year 1500," Botticelli wrote, "during the troubles of Italy . . . which was prophesied in . . . the Apocalypse, when the devil was loosed upon the earth . . . and we shall see him trodden underfoot as in this picture."

# THE NATIVITY

THE NATIONAL GALLERY, LONDON

*Reproduced by courtesy of the Trustees*

Botticelli hobbled about his studio giving directions to his assistants. He was fifty-seven years old, but he looked much older. He no longer painted big pictures, but when he felt strong enough, worked on a set of little panels for a chest. On each panel he showed scenes from the life of Saint Zenobius. One showed the saint performing three different miracles. On the left he brought a dead youth to life. In the center he revived a messenger who had been killed. Inside a building on the right the saint handed a cup of holy water to a priest, who then rushed across the square to bless a relative who was dying. A background of cold stone buildings, broken by a barren landscape made the plunging figures look more violent.

While Botticelli painted quietly in his studio, young Michelangelo was furiously carving an enormous statue in his workshop. People passing the shed where he worked heard the ring of hammer and chisel as he chipped away pieces of marble. When the statue was finished the governors appointed a group of Florence's best artists to decide where Michelangelo's David should be placed. Botticelli, walking painfully on crutches, met with the other artists. When the committee could not agree, Michelangelo was asked to choose the spot. A few days later the church bells of Florence rang out, while the giant statue of David was placed in the public square.

Botticelli's assistants continued to fill orders for religious paintings, but Sandro no longer felt strong enough to visit his workshop. He and Simone lived quietly in their country villa, until in the spring of 1510, Sandro Botticelli died. He was sixty-six years old. He was buried in the graveyard of the Church of Ognissanti next to the house where he had lived and worked. Many people did not know that the artist who was buried that day had once been the most popular painter in Florence. Other artists had come to take his place. But Botticelli's spirit is alive today in his paintings of graceful nymphs, dancing angels and melancholy Madonnas.

**THREE MIRACLES OF SAINT ZENOBIUS**

# BIBLIOGRAPHY

Alexandre, Arsène: *Botticelli*. Paris, Les Editions Rieder, 1929

Anderson, A. J: *The Romance of Sandro Botticelli*. New York, Dodd Mead & Co., 1912

Argan, Guilio Carlo: *Botticelli*, Etude Biographique et Critique. Editions d'art Albert Skira, Genève, Paris, New York, 1957

Binns, Henry Bryan: *Botticelli*. London, T. C. & E. C. Jack; New York, Frederick A. Stokes, 1907

Bode, Wilhelm: *Sandro Botticelli*. Translated by Renfield & F. L. Rudston Brown, London, Methuen & Co. Ltd., 1925

*Botticelli. Drawings for Dante's Inferno*. New York, Lear, 1947

Brion, Marcel: *Botticelli*. Paris, Les Editions G. Gres & Cie., 1937

Cartwright, Julia: *Sandro Botticelli*. London, Duckworth & Co.; New York, E. P. Dutton & Co.

Chastel, André: *Botticelli*. Greenwich, Conn., New York Graphic Society, 1958

Cleugh, James: *Tuscan Spring*. New York, Reynal & Hitchcock, 1939

Collison-Morley, L.: *The Early Medici*. New York, E. P. Dutton & Co. Inc., 1936

Cust, R. H., Hobart, M. A.: *Botticelli*. London, George Bell & Sons, 1908

Diehl, Charles: *Botticelli*. Paris, Librairie de l'art Ancien et Moderne

*Drawings by Sandro Botticelli for Dante's Divina Commedia*. Commentary by F. Lippmann, London, Lawrence & Bollen, 1896

Eisler, Dr. Robert: *Botticelli, La Derelitta*. Art and Reason, April, 1939

Hennessy, John Pope: *Botticelli, The Nativity*. London, Percy, Lund, Humphries & Co. Ltd. Publishers

Horne, Herbert P.: *Sandro Botticelli, Painter of Florence*. London, George Bell & Sons, 1908, 2 vol.

Hubbard, Elbert: *Little Journeys to the Homes of Eminent Artists. Botticelli*. East Aurora, New York, Roycrofters, 1902

Loth, David: *Lorenzo the Magnificent*. New York, Brentano's, 1929

Mesnil, Jacques: *Botticelli*. Albin Michel, Editeur, Paris, 1938

Richter, J. P.: *Lectures on the National Gallery*. London, Longmans, Green and Co., 1898

Ridolphi, Roberto: *The Life of Girolamo Savonarola*. Translated from the Italian by Cecil Grayson, London, Routledge & Kegan Paul, 1957

Roeder, Ralph: *The Man of the Renaissance*. New York, The Viking Press, 1933

Schaeffer, E.: *Sandro Botticelli*. Translated by Francis F. Cox. New York, Frederick A. Stokes Co.

Schneider, René: *Botticelli*, Biographie Critique, Paris Librairie Renouard. Henri Laurens, Editeur

Spender, Stephen: *Botticelli*. Pitman Publishing Corp. New York, London, 1948

Steinmann, Ernst: *Botticelli*. Translated by Campbell Dodgson. New York, Lemcke & Buechner, 1901

Streeter, A.: *Botticelli*. London, George Bell and Sons, 1907

Terrasse, Charles: *Botticelli*. Librairie Renouard. Henri Laurens, Editeur, 1935
Venturi, Lionello: *Botticelli*. Vienna, The Phaidon Press, London, George Allen & Unwin Ltd., 1937
Wind, Edgar: *The Subject of Botticelli's Derelitta*. Journal of the Warburg & Courtauld Institutes, Vol. IV, 1940-41
Yashiro, Yukio: *Sandro Botticelli* and the Florentine Renaissance. Boston, Hale, Cushman and Flint; London, The Medici Society Ltd., 1929
Young, Col. G. F., C. B.: *The Medici*. New York, The Modern Library, 1930

# INDEX